Cruelty /
Killing Floor

Cruelty /
Killing Floor

POEMS BY Ai

Foreword by Carolyn Forché

THUNDER'S
MOUTH
PRESS
NEW YORK

Published in the United States by
Thunder's Mouth Press, 93–99 Greene Street, New York, N.Y. 10012
Cover design by Loretta Li
Grateful acknowledgement is made to
the New York State Council on the Arts
and the National Endowment for the Arts for
financial assistance with the publication of this work.
Grateful acknowledgement is made to the
John Simon Guggenheim Memorial Foundation,
The Radcliffe Institute, and the Massachusetts
Arts and Humanities Foundation, without whose
help *Killing Floor* might never have been finished.
Reprinted by special arrangement with Houghton Mifflin
Some of the poems in this volume have previously appeared
in various magazines, as follows:
American Poetry Review, Antaeus, Black Box, Chicago Review,
Choice, Exile, Iowa Review, Ironwood, Lillabullero,
Michigan Quarterly Review, Paris Review, Renaissance,
and *Virginia Quarterly Review.*
Library of Congress Cataloging-in-Publication Data
Ai, 1947–
Cruelty ; Killing floor.
(Classic reprint series)
Reprint (1st work). Originally published:
Boston : Houghton Mifflin, 1973.
Reprint (2nd work). Originally published:
Boston : Houghton Mifflin, 1979.
I. Ai, 1947– . Killing floor. 1987. II. Title.
III. Title: Killing floor. IV. Series.
PS3551.I2A6 1987 811'.54 86-23192
ISBN 0-938410-38-5 (pbk.)
Distributed by PERSEA BOOKS INC.
225 Lafayette, New York, N.Y. 10012
212-431-5270
Manufactured in the United States of America

CONTENTS

Cruelty

Killing Floor

FOREWORD

Against a landscape of salt flats, fields, interstates and wind-blown clapboards, a truck squats low on four flat tires. A boy circles it with an iron rod and there is only the ringing of rod on metal and the disembodied voice of the boy's father as his family pauses for a tableau of terror. The boy kills his father first, then his mother and sister. He is "The Kid" who hits the road, dressed in his father's best clothes, carrying in a suitcase his mother's nightgown, his sister's doll. "The Kid" closes with: "I'm fourteen. I'm a wind from nowhere./I can break your heart."

In *Killing Floor*—the 1978 Lamont Poetry Selection of the American Academy of Poets, Ai's voice joins with that of a German soldier marching through Russia, who imagines eating the "terrible luminous eyes" of Adolf Hitler. This chorus of personae also includes a woman who slaughters her own children, a boy who makes love to a corpse, a woman who sells herself, and a man who commits hari-kari and then climbs the chords of his own entrails into heaven. There is Lope de Aguirre, who in 1561 attempted to conquer Peru "with his soul between his teeth," and who closes this book with a message to the deity: "God. The boot heel an inch above your head is mine./ God, say your prayers."

Who else but Ai, born of Native America, Africa and Asia, could so address the deity, with such defiance? Who other than the poet who gave us *Cruelty* fourteen years ago, speaking not for the distanced self but the dispossessed, would have the right? There had not been a poetry more sexual, nor a poet braver in showing us how she could "cut through life like a diamond/in a sack of glass." Encountering her work was for me like coming upon a campfire on the outskirts of town built by a woman who could tell me everything I needed to know. On this "black tire, Earth" we were beginning the twentieth-century decline and in the years to come we would need to know what went on in the minds of those who had suffered the most. *Cruelty* showed us where the rifles and knives were hidden, and beginning with our blood-washed births, what might be expected of a tenancy on earth.

From Russia, Mexico, Buchenwald and Minnesota, the voices speak of patricide, necrophilia, self-immolation, cannibalism and torture, converging in the single voice of an old soul, androgynous and driving, a ghost ranging space and time, drawn to moments in which the oppressed one is moved to act. Ai is concerned with that single moment, revelatory and disassociated, which is the hinge of human history, facilitating radical change, allowing the heart to open to a new order.

She discovers that it is possible to enter a psychological state of anarchy (symbolic always of social anarchy) without becoming hysterical. These poems are cold-blooded, tender and defiant narratives, concerning themselves with the survival of the human will, and a deferential celebration of death as a magnifier of life.

In many of her poems, there are knives, axes, blades or pitchforks, splitting skulls, slicing off pieces of flesh, jabbing the sun. Their cutting edges become, in this poet's hands, instruments for penetrating a social order which has become anesthetized to human agony.

In counterpoint, there are images of women lifting their skirts, just as darkness lifts its own, revealing the feminine, revealing daylight. There is constant repetition of burning, of fire and light: the bullet holes in Zapata's body are "black, eight-pointed stars," that "gave off a luminous darkness." In a primitive act of exorcism, a coffin containing a doll is burned: "I laugh. The boy dances and I follow him,/ 'round and 'round, two black tops on fire,/ spinning under a sky full of firecrackers and stars,/ letting fall a few handkerchiefs of light."

So it is that because of the belief in both death and life, there are no senseless acts. In the human spirit's endurance, revolution is possible and transformation, inevitable.

Ai as Emiliano Zapata climbs a hill, and begins cutting "rows and rows of black corn." When the stalks touch the field, "they turn into men." The poet/Zapata shouts: "Dying doesn't end anything./ Get up. Swing those machetes./ You can't steal a man's glory/ without a goddamned fight./ Boys, take the land, take it; it's yours./ If you suffer in the grave,/ you can kill from it."

There aren't many poets whose language so precisely resonates with the pervasive concerns of the contemporary human condition.

CAROLYN FORCHÉ

Cruelty

TWENTY-YEAR MARRIAGE

You keep me waiting in a truck
with its one good wheel stuck in the ditch,
while you piss against the south side of a tree.
Hurry. I've got nothing on under my skirt tonight.
That still excites you, but this pickup has no windows
and the seat, one fake leather thigh,
pressed close to mine is cold.
I'm the same size, shape, make as twenty years ago,
but get inside me, start the engine;
you'll have the strength, the will to move.
I'll pull, you push, we'll tear each other in half.
Come on, baby, lay me down on my back.
Pretend you don't owe me a thing
and maybe we'll roll out of here,
leaving the past stacked up behind us;
old newspapers nobody's ever got to read again.

ABORTION

Coming home, I find you still in bed,
but when I pull back the blanket,
I see your stomach is flat as an iron.
You've done it, as you warned me you would
and left the fetus wrapped in wax paper
for me to look at. My son.
Woman, loving you no matter what you do,
what can I say, except that I've heard
the poor have no children, just small people
and there is room only for one man in this house.

THE COUNTRY MIDWIFE:
A DAY

I bend over the woman.
This is the third time between abortions.
I dip a towel into a bucket of hot water
and catch the first bit of blood,
as the blue-pink dome of a head breaks through.
A scraggy, red child comes out of her into my hands
like warehouse ice sliding down the chute.

It's done, the stink of birth, Old Grizzly
rears up on his hind legs in front of me
and I want to go outside,
but the air smells the same there too.
The woman's left eye twitches
and beneath her, a stain as orange as sunrise
spreads over the sheet.
I lift my short, blunt fingers to my face
and I let her bleed, Lord, I let her bleed.

THE UNEXPECTED

As I wipe the dust off my face,
you sweep the kitchen floor
for the third time today
and I wonder if we are having some special guest.
I don't feel like company,
but I know it doesn't bother you, woman,
pregnant walnut of flesh,
waiting for birth to crack you open
with her sharp, brown teeth
and force you to give up your white meat.

You sweep the dirt into a pile.
I get the dustpan and kneel down,
so you can push the dirt onto it,
but before you've finished,
I reach under your skirt and stroke your ankle.
It's wet. Frightened, I stand up.
Go on, just give me the broom
and let me finish sweeping up for you,
you never know who might stop by
and everything's got to be clean, clean.

BUT WHAT I'M TRYING TO SAY MOTHER IS

You are barely able to walk,
sewn up between your legs, bleeding,
and slumped over from the weight
of six months of pregnancy,
although it *is* all over.
You wear your green chenille robe
and carry a picture of the dead child, the fifth one.
Mother, why don't you stop looking at me?
Let me wash you, please.
And yes, I go to the cemetery.
I cry, I pray for his soul,
I pour milk on his grave,
and I do it because I loved you once, I did
and it was good.

THE ESTRANGED

I lay peeled potatoes in the iron pot,
beside the meat, as it strains a tongue of fat
to lick its own blood,
just as I strain at keeping you with me.
I am the needle, woman,
let me pierce your camel eye
and sew you to me with iron thread,
let my ovaries, the potatoes,
give you a bridge of babies' heads
to cross back into yourself
and my monthly blood, mixed with water,
will be a blanket of gravy to cover you
from one icy night to the next.

CRUELTY

The hoof-marks on the dead wildcat
gleam in the dark.
You are naked, as you drag it up on the porch.
That won't work either.
Drinking ice water hasn't,
nor having the bedsprings snap fingers
to help us keep rhythm.
I've never once felt anything
that might get close. Can't you see?
The thing I want most is hard,
running toward my own teeth
and it bites back.

THE TENANT FARMER

Hailstones puncture the ground,
as I sit at the table, rubbing a fork.
My woman slides a knife across her lips,
then lays it beside a cup of water.
Each day she bites another notch in her thumb
and I pretend relief is coming
as the smooth black tire, Earth,
wheels around the sun without its patch of topsoil
and my mouth speaks: *wheat, barley, red cabbage,*
roll on home to Jesus,
it's too late now you're dead.

STARVATION

Rain, tobacco juice, spit from the sky
shatters against your body,
as you push the pane of glass through the mud.
The white oak frame of the house shakes
when I slam the door and stand on the porch,
fanning myself with a piece of cardboard,
cut in the shape of a ham.

There's a pot of air on the stove.
You drove seventy miles, paid for that glass
and I can't remember the last good meal I had,
but bring it up here. I'll help you. I'm not angry.
We'll paint the sun on it from the inside,
so if we die some night, a light will still be on.
It's hell to starve in the dark.
I don't know why. I'm just your woman,
like you, crazy to lose all I've got.
It's rotten, you know, rotten.
The table's set. What time is it?
Wash your hands first. You're late.

PROSTITUTE

Husband, for a while, after I shoot you,
I don't touch your body,
I just cool it with my paper fan,
the way I used to on hot nights,
as the moon rises, chip of avocado

and finally, too bored to stay any longer,
I search your pockets, finding a few coins.
I slip your hand under my skirt
and rub it against my chili-red skin,
then I put on your black boots.
I stick the gun in my waistband,
two beaded combs in my hair.

I never cost much,
but tonight, with a gun, your boots . . .

POSSESSIONS

You sit on the porch steps,
rubbing your knuckles on your pants.
I press the hen against my skirt
and go into the kitchen.
As I slice through the right wing,
I hear you come inside, and soon, your mouth is on my arm.
I wait for you to ask me how it was with the other man,
but you don't need to.
You have it all now, even what was his.

WHY CAN'T I LEAVE YOU?

You stand behind the old black mare,
dressed as always in that red shirt,
stained from sweat, the crying of the armpits,
that will not stop for anything,
stroking her rump, while the barley goes unplanted.
I pick up my suitcase and set it down,
as I try to leave you again.
I smooth the hair back from your forehead.
I think, with your laziness and the drought too,
you'll be needing my help more than ever.
You take my hands, I nod
and go to the house to unpack,
having found another reason to stay.

I undress, then put on my white lace slip
for you to take off, because you like that
and when you come in, you pull down the straps
and I unbutton your shirt.
I know we can't give each other any more
or any less than what we have.
There is safety in that, so much
that I can never get past the packing,
the begging you to please, if I can't make you happy,
come close between my thighs
and let me laugh for you from my second mouth.

*knows she's
stuck - relati
can't go
anywhere*

12

I HAVE GOT TO STOP
LOVING YOU

So I have killed my black goat.
His kidney floats in a bowl,
a beige, flat fish, around whom parasites, slices of lemon,
break through the surface of hot broth, then sink below,
as I bend, face down in the steam, breathing in.
I hear this will cure anything.

When I am finished, I walk up to him.
He hangs from a short wooden post,
tongue stuck out of his mouth,
tasting the hay-flavored air.
A bib of flies gather at his throat
and further down, where he is open
and bare of all his organs,
I put my hand in, stroke him once,
then taking it out, look at the sky.
The stormclouds there break open
and raindrops, yellow as black cats' eyes, come down
each a tiny river, hateful and alone.

Wishing I could get out of this alive, I hug myself.
It is hard to remember if he suffered much.

YOUNG FARM WOMAN ALONE

What could I do with a man? —
pull him on like these oxhide boots,
the color of plums, dipped in blue ink
and stomp hell out of my loneliness,
this hoe that with each use grows sharper.

RECAPTURE

When you run off, I start after you,
as the sun rolls overhead
and rocks in the sky's blue hands.

As always, I find you, beat you.
The corner of your mouth bleeds
and your tongue slips out, slips in.
You don't fight me, you never do.

Going back, you stumble against me
and I grab your wrist, pulling you down.
Come on, bitch of my love, while it is still easy.

WOMAN TO MAN

Lightning hits the roof,
shoves the knife, darkness,
deep in the walls.
They bleed light all over us
and your face, the fan, folds up,
so I won't see how afraid
to be with me you are.
We don't mix, even in bed,
where we keep ending up.
There's no need to hide it:
you're snow, I'm coal,
I've got the scars to prove it.
But open your mouth,
I'll give you a taste of black
you won't forget.
For a while, I'll let it make you strong,
make your heart lion,
then I'll take it back.

THE ANNIVERSARY

You raise the ax,
the block of wood screams in half,
while I lift the sack of flour
and carry it into the house.
I'm not afraid of the blade
you've just pointed at my head.
If I were dead, you could take the boy,
hunt, kiss gnats, instead of my moist lips.
Take it easy, squabs are roasting,
corn, still in husks, crackles,
as the boy dances around the table:
old guest at a wedding party for two sad-faced clowns,
who together, never won a round of anything but hard times.
Come in, sheets are clean,
fall down on me for one more year
and we can blast another hole in ourselves without a sound.

1931

I bend to kiss your breasts, but you push me away
and I go to the bedroom to look at my son.
His irises, two blue, baby onions
come apart as he wakes.
I take him to you and walk into the street.
I can't blame you for not wanting me.
Before you only gave yourself out of boredom
and with this hunger, even that is gone.
I hear the screen door slam and keep walking.
I know you'll follow, always behind or ahead of me,
never at my side.

TIRED OLD WHORE

This is my property, I laid for it, paid for it, you know,
and I just want to build a cement walkway
right up to my front door.
I'll be the only whore within fifty miles
who can claim she did something with her hands
that didn't get a man hard.

What? — but I'm so tired. Can't you wait a while?
I'm forty-five, my breath's short, I like to sleep alone.
Yeah, yeah, I rolled in my jelly and it felt good,
but this belly isn't wood, or steel.
Man, turn your butt to my face.
But wait, I need a little help, help me, sweet thing.
Pull down your pants.
I like to see what I'm getting now,
before it gets into me.

FORTY-THREE-YEAR-OLD WOMAN, MASTURBATING

I want to kill this female hand —
its four centipede fingers;
the thumb, cricket, that lags behind,
digging its nail into me, until I move my legs apart;
the palm, body of a tarantula,
that sinks down over my clitoris,
as the fingers inch into my vagina —
but each time, after it happens,
the fingers, moist and flaccid, crawl up to my mouth,
my grasshopper tongue, darting out, licks them
and I am grateful for a small taste of anything.

OLD WOMAN, YOUNG MAN

He thrusts his arms in the barrel of grain,
takes them out
and rubs them across his bare chest
because I love the gritty feel of it
and wear it on each breast like a bracelet.

Unashamed, I part my legs.
As always he says, *look there's a rose,*
yes, but it's lost its teeth.
He eats without tasting
and I reach to scratch my name
on the damp face rising
with a few crinkled gray hairs
shoving their white-tipped heads
against his scarred and frightened lips.

ONE MAN DOWN

Your brother brings you home from hunting,
slung over your horse, dead,
with the wild boar tied down beside you.
I ask no questions.

He throws the boar at my feet,
hands me the red licorice he promised.
I drop my shawl
and his hands cover my breasts.
He whispers of a dress in town,
while I unbutton my skirt.

I sit on the ground, waiting,
while he loosens his belt.
He smiles, swings it across my face,
then pushes me back. I keep my eyes open.
The hound's paws bloody the tiles
lining the flower bed.
The bitch walks behind him, licking his tracks.
I scratch the flesh above me.
The odor of fresh meat
digs a finger in my nostrils.
The horse rears,
your body slides from the black saddle
like a bedroll of fine velvet.
I laugh, close my eyes, and relax.

AFTER A LONG TIME

the halves of the egg, impotence,
slide into each other on waxed feet
and the wait is over.
The seam between my legs
basted with hair tears apart,
as your blue, flannel spoon slips inside,
digs out the pieces of cracked shell
and lays them on my thighs,
like old china plates made too thin
for holding anything but love.

HANGMAN

In the fields, the silos open their mouths
and let the grain dribble down their sides,
for they are overflowing.
The farmers swing their scythes, brows dripping blood.
They have had the passion ripped out of their chests
and share no brotherhood with the wheat,

while far across the open land,
the Hangman mounts an empty scaffold.
He slides his hands over the coarse-grained cedar
and smells the whole Lebanese coast
in the upraised arms of Kansas.
The rope's stiff bristles prick his fingers,
as he holds it and lifts himself above the trap door.

He touches the wood again.
This will be his last hanging
and anyway he has seen other fields,
workmen nailing brass spikes into the scaffolds
and rope which coiled and uncoiled
in the laps of farm women.
He places his foot on the step going down
and nearby, a scarecrow explodes,
sending tiny slivers of straw into his eyes.

THE SWEET

The man steps in out of the blizzard with his Klootch,
his Eskimo prostitute and the room heats up, as they
cross the floor. I know he is dying and I spin a half
dollar around on the bar, then slide my eyes over the woman.
She has a seal's body. Her face is a violet in the center
of the moon. The half dollar falls over, I remind myself
that to love a Klootch is always to be filled with emptiness,
turn and lift my glass.

I shake my head, drink. When I hear retreating footsteps,
I turn. The man stands at the door, facing me. His hand
gropes out, as the woman backs off and I see the Northern
Lights flare up in his eyes, before he stumbles and falls.
The woman leans back against the wall. I pick up the half
dollar, spin it around again and go to her. We walk out
into the darkness and I am cold as I squeeze her buttocks,
her blue, dwarf stars.

THE COLOR THIEF

I enter your room,
with my purple face moist from excitement.
The black straw basket I carry
in my yellow arms cracks softly,
in tune with the brittle snap of my blue legs,
as I sneak to your bed.
Little girl, have you got a pink buttock to lend,
or a cream-colored navel
that darkens to brown as it spirals inward?

Or breasts? Yes.
They are swelling now
for the first time.
I touch them.
I take the nipples in my hands.
They are hard
and almost as magenta as plums.
I drop them into my basket
and leave quickly.
The light bulbs I've stuck in the tips of your breasts
shine far into your middle age,
the clearest white I've ever seen.

THE CORPSE HAULER'S ELEGY

Beside the river, I stop the wagon,
loaded with the plague dead
and have a drink.
I fill my mouth and swallow slowly,
then climb back into my seat.
The old horse drops one turd, another.
Corpses, I give you these flowers.

THE HITCHHIKER

The Arizona wind dries out my nostrils
and the heat of the sidewalk burns my shoes,
as a woman drives up slowly.
I get in, grinning at a face I do not like,
but I slide my arm across the top of the seat
and rest it lightly against her shoulder.
We turn off into the desert,
then I reach inside my pocket and touch the switchblade.

We stop, and as she moves closer to me, my hands ache,
but somehow, I get the blade into her chest.
I think a song: "Everybody needs somebody,
everybody needs somebody to love,"
as the black numerals 35 roll out of her right eye
inside one small tear.
Laughing, I snap my fingers. Rape, murder, I got you
in the sight of my gun.

I move off toward the street.
My feet press down in it,
familiar with the hot, soft asphalt
that caresses them.
The sun slips down into its cradle behind the mountains
and it is hot, hotter than ever
and I like it.

THE ROOT EATER

The war has begun
and I see the Root Eater bending,
shifting his hands under the soil
in search of the arthritic knuckles of trees.
I see dazed flower stems
pushing themselves back into the ground.
I see turnips spinning endlessly
on the blunt, bitten-off tips of their noses.
I see the Root Eater going home on his knees,
full of the ripe foundations of things,
longing to send his seed up through his feet
and out into the morning

but the stumps of trees heave themselves forward
for the last march
and the Root Eater waits,
knowing he will be shoved, rootless,
under the brown, scaly torso of the rock.

THE WIDOW

After I burn the boar's carcass,
I fill the slop bucket
and the old sow gets up,
grunting from deep inside,
where the piglets, just beginning to wake,
are already smelling the sour food,
and stretching their pink toes toward me.

As I dump the slop into the trough,
the sow rubs her snout against my leg
and I kneel, pushing my head through
to the muddy side of her body.
I touch her teat with my tongue.
She grunts and I climb over the fence.
I sink down on my side
in the mud, the wet, black cotton of the earth,
as my wife calls. No, not my wife, the woman.
I don't say anything.
How can I tell her he will never come?

THE DESERTER

Through the hole in the hut's wall,
I watch the old woman who put me up,
leaning against a wooden tub, elbow deep in wash water.
I go to her, feeling an itch somewhere inside my mouth,
knowing I've got to leave everything of myself here.
I raise the rifle, as she presses a white shawl
far down in the water, and fire.
She dies quietly; even her heart spits blood
through clenched teeth.

I take bread, onions, radishes and set out,
leaving my rifle behind, while the wind is down
and stillness, with its knives of powdered lead,
slashes the coarse, brown hair from my arms
as I hold them, empty, at my sides.

CUBA, 1962

When the rooster jumps up on the windowsill
and spreads his red-gold wings,
I wake, thinking it is the sun
and call Juanita, hearing her answer,
but only in my mind.
I know she is already outside,
breaking the cane off at ground level,
using only her big hands.
I get the machete and walk among the cane,
until I see her, lying face-down in the dirt.

Juanita, dead in the morning like this.
I raise the machete —
what I take from the earth, I give back —
and cut off her feet.
I lift the body and carry it to the wagon,
where I load the cane to sell in the village.
Whoever tastes my woman in his candy, his cake,
tastes something sweeter than this sugar cane;
it is grief.
If you eat too much of it, you want more,
you can never get enough.

SUNDAY

changeling, props a coffin against my door,
stains the windows with its brown curtains,
floats, belly-up in my glass of water.
I see its back in my mirror,
its hand walking in my shoes.
I smell its piss odor in my underwear
and when it peels off the sheet onto my body,
I yell, grab for its throat
and get its mud heart, shaped like a box,
and just full of things
you can't quite put your finger on.

INDECISION

seamstress, you sew a screen door to my mouth
and it slams back against my cheek, soundlessly,
when I try to speak,
leaving only a question mark
that wheels around on its period,
its one leg, yelling, go ahead,
ask me anything, ask me anything,
but don't make me decide what to do.

THE CRIPPLE

I pull my legs from the floor,
as I would two weeds, gently,
pretending my roots have remained
in the soil that once held me upright
in the palm of its hand,
in the roads of black thread,
I walked, sowing years.
Instead, the itch deep in my heel
cries from its mouth one thorn after another.

THE SUICIDE

The street coughs blood
in a linen handkerchief,
as I strut down to the river,
where the oil ships, black bars of soap,
float upright on steel spines.
The wharf has a tight, deep vagina of water
and I'm going to fuck it until it novas,
just to let everybody see
how I cut through life like a diamond
in a sack of glass, with no regrets,
and a what's it to you
to shove up your ass.

DISREGARD

Overhead, the match burns out,
but the chunk of ice in the back seat
keeps melting from imagined heat,
while the old Hudson tiptoes up the slope.
My voile blouse, so wet it is transparent,
like one frightened hand, clutches my chest.
The bag of rock salt sprawled beside me wakes, thirsty
and stretches a shaky tongue toward the ice.

I press the gas pedal hard.
I'll get back to the house, the dirt yard, the cesspool,
to you out back, digging a well
you could fill with your sweat,
though there is not one reason I should want to.
You never notice me until the end of the day,
when your hand is on my knee
and the ice cream, cooked to broth,
is hot enough to burn the skin off my touch.

CHILD BEATER

Outside, the rain, pinafore of gray water, dresses the town
and I stroke the leather belt,
as she sits in the rocking chair,
holding a crushed paper cup to her lips.
I yell at her, but she keeps rocking;
back, her eyes open, forward, they close.
Her body, somehow fat, though I feed her only once a day,
reminds me of my own just after she was born.
It's been seven years, but I still can't forget how I felt.
How heavy it feels to look at her.

I lay the belt on a chair
and get her dinner bowl.
I hit the spoon against it, set it down
and watch her crawl to it,
pausing after each forward thrust of her legs
and when she takes her first bite,
I grab the belt and beat her across the back
until her tears, beads of salt-filled glass, falling,
shatter on the floor.

I move off. I let her eat,
while I get my dog's chain leash from the closet.
I whirl it around my head.
O daughter, so far, you've only had a taste of icing,
are you ready now for some cake?

THE DWARF

From where I stand, Fat Lady,
I can see you winding the radium clock
in your vagina,
while your half-life, already caught in the lymph nodes
is burning out.
I can see the pimples on your knees growing red,
hairs sprouting, split at the tips, each a great antenna,
your toes wiggling in despair
and there in your eyes, my own shoe-like face,
laced with the same uncontrollable laughter.

WARRIOR

You sharpen the tip of spear
with your teeth,
while your wife plows the ground
with jawbone of an ox.
She is a great, black fire.

The old blood is drifting up your throat
and the witch-men sing all night
of melon-breasted women in rival villages,
but the spear is wilting in your hands.

When you are standing in the river,
you grab a fish,
tear its flesh open with your teeth, and hold it,
until the bones in your fingers break up
and fly about you like moths.

The river, a fish, your fingers, moths,
the war song churning in your belly.

WOMAN

The adobe walls of the house
clutch the noon heat in tin fists
and while bathing, I fan my breasts,
watching the nipples harden.
I pinch them, feeling nothing, but wanting to,
and shift my weight from left buttock to right,
while the water circling my waist tightens,
as if you had commanded it.
I stand up, spreading my legs apart,
ready to release the next ribbon of blood.

All right. You want me now, this way.
I haven't locked the door.
My swollen belly feels only its heaviness,
you would weigh less than the pain
chipping away at my navel with an ice pick of muscle.
I can carry you.
The blood, halved and thinned, rolls down my legs,
cupping each foot in a red stirrup
and I am riding that invisible horse,
the same one my mother rode.
It's hungry, it has to be fed,
the last man couldn't, can you?

THE RIVALS

You swat flies with your hand, cursing,
calling them the names of our sons.
Forget them, we don't need them to help us.
On days when you drive the wagon into town
I wear the harness myself and keep plowing.
Some nights, too, while sleeping, I dream you young again,
shoving your snake up me, hissing the love
you can never say you feel
and wake to find your fingers
combing the snarled hair between my legs,
until I rise up on one arm, twenty years your junior,
moan for more and get a back turned to my eyes.
I take the old, smoked sausage from under my pillow
and push it inside me, before I tell you
how much of a woman I still am.

I go out to the wagon,
where I am painting roses; ten on two sides,
one for the pencil, each year,
that drew a black line across my face
since you first laid me beneath you.
It's true my back's bent, my breasts smell like buttermilk.
You used to love that, but I understand.
I'm the first woman you had,
I've got the saw mark across my leg
where you brought it down on me, when I was heavy-bellied,
unable to help you with the chores.

Now you kill flies, your body rains sweat, you wet your pants
if I don't get them down in time.
Holding the bucket of paint, I dance and sing.
You think you can walk a step without stumbling, you
                                          sonofabitch?
Just try it. Fall! I don't give a damn.
You're hurting, so am I,
but I'm strong enough to let you cry alone.

EVERYTHING: ELOY,
ARIZONA, 1956

Tin shack, where my baby sleeps on his back
the way the hound taught him;
highway, black zebra, with one white stripe;
nickel in my pocket for chewing gum;
you think you're all I've got.
But when the 2 ton rolls to a stop
and the driver gets out,
I sit down in the shade and wave each finger,
saving my whole hand till the last.

He's keys, tires, a fire lit in his belly
in the diner up the road.
I'm red toenails, tight blue halter, black slip.
He's mine tonight. I don't know him.
He can only hurt me a piece at a time.

BEFORE YOU LEAVE

I set the bowl of raw vegetables on the table.
You know I am ripe now.
You can bite me, I won't bleed;
just take off my kimono. Eat, then go ahead, run.
I won't miss you, but this one hour
lift me by the buttocks
and press me hard against your belly.
Fill my tunnel with the howl
you keep zipped in your pants
and when it's over, don't worry, I'll stand.
I'm a mare. Every nail's head
in my hooves wears your face,
but not even you, wolf, can bring me down.

NEW CROPS FOR A FREE MAN

I drop the torch of rags in a bucket of water,
then watch the field burn.

Behind me, another fire, my woman,
under sheets wrinkled and stiff from heat and sweat,
throws them back and rises.
She cracks her knuckles, leans from the window and yells,
but I keep my head turned toward the thing I understand.
She's hot from a match I never lit
and strokes her breasts, cone-shaped candles,
whose wicks, her nipples, aflame, burn holes in her hands, in me.

Go back to sleep, I don't need you now.
I just want the dirt under my fingernails to become mountains,
to listen to my heartbeat inside the rocks
and scream as my own death slides into bed
with her ass bloody and sweet when I lick it,
one stalk of wheat no man
can pull from the ground and live to eat.

Killing Floor

for the ghosts

KILLING FLOOR

1. Russia, 1927

On the day the sienna-skinned man
held my shoulders between his spade-shaped hands,
easing me down into the azure water of Jordan,
I woke ninety-three million miles from myself,
Lev Davidovich Bronstein,
shoulder-deep in the Volga,
while the cheap dye of my black silk shirt darkened the water.

My head wet, water caught in my lashes.
Am I blind?
I rub my eyes, then wade back to shore,
undress and lie down,
until Stalin comes from his place beneath the birch tree.
He folds my clothes
and I button myself in my marmot coat,
and together we start the long walk back to Moscow.
He doesn't ask, *what did you see in the river?*,
but I hear the hosts of a man drowning in water and holiness,
the castrati voices I can't recognize,
skating on knives, from trees, from air
on the thin ice of my last night in Russia.
Leon Trotsky. Bread.
I want to scream, but silence holds my tongue
with small spade-shaped hands
and only this comes, so quietly

Stalin has to press his ear to my mouth:
I have only myself. Put me on the train.
I won't look back.

2. Mexico, 1940

At noon today, I woke from a nightmare:
my friend Jacques ran toward me with an ax,
as I stepped from the train in Alma-Ata.
He was dressed in yellow satin pants and shirt.
A marigold in winter.
When I held out my arms to embrace him,
he raised the ax and struck me at the neck,
my head fell to one side, hanging only by skin.
A river of sighs poured from the cut.

3. Mexico, August 20, 1940

The machine-gun bullets
hit my wife in the legs,
then zigzagged up her body.
I took the shears, cut open her gown
and lay on top of her for hours.
Blood soaked through my clothes
and when I tried to rise, I couldn't.

I wake then. Another nightmare.
I rise from my desk, walk to the bedroom

and sit down at my wife's mirrored vanity.
I rouge my cheeks and lips,
stare at my bone-white, speckled egg of a face:
lined and empty.
I lean forward and see Jacques's reflection.
I half-turn, smile, then turn back to the mirror.
He moves from the doorway,
lifts the pickax
and strikes the top of my head.
My brain splits.
The pickax keeps going
and when it hits the tile floor,
it flies from his hands,
a black dove on whose back I ride,
two men, one cursing,
the other blessing all things:
Lev Davidovich Bronstein,
I step from Jordan without you.

NOTHING BUT COLOR

For Yukio Mishima

I didn't write Etsuko,
I sliced her open.
She was carmine inside
like a sea bass
and empty.
No viscera, nothing but color.
I love you like that, boy.
I pull the kimono down around your shoulders
and kiss you.
Then you let it fall open.
Each time, I cut you a little
and when you leave, I take the piece,
broil it, dip it in ginger sauce
and eat it. It burns my mouth so.
You laugh, holding me belly-down
with your body.
So much hurting to get to this moment,
when I'm beneath you,
wanting it to go on and to end.

At midnight, you say *see you tonight*
and I answer *there won't be any tonight*,
but you just smile, swing your sweater
over your head and tie the sleeves around your neck.
I hear you whistling long after you disappear
down the subway steps,

as I walk back home, my whole body tingling.
I undress
and put the bronze sword on my desk
beside the crumpled sheet of rice paper.
I smooth it open
and read its single sentence:
I meant to do it.
No. It should be common and feminine
like *I can't go on sharing him,*
or something to imply that.
Or the truth:
that I saw in myself
the five signs of the decay of the angel
and you were holding on, watching and free,
that I decided to go out
with the pungent odor
of this cold and consuming passion in my nose: death.
Now, I've said it. That vulgar word
that drags us down to the worms, sightless, predestined.
Goddamn you, boy.
Nothing I said mattered to you;
that bullshit about Etsuko or about killing myself.
I tear the note, then burn it.
The alarm clock goes off. 5:45 A.M.
I take the sword and walk into the garden.
I look up. The sun, the moon,
two round teeth rock together

and the light of one chews up the other.
I stab myself in the belly,
wait, then stab myself again. Again.
It's snowing. I'll turn to ice,
but I'll burn anyone who touches me.
I start pulling my guts out,
those red silk cords,
spiraling skyward,
and I'm climbing them
past the moon and the sun,
past darkness
into white.
I mean to live.

LESSON, LESSON

I draw a circle on a paper bag
with the only crayon you've ever had
and hold it above the cot.
You laugh. So the sun ain't green.
You not supposed to know yet.
Just pretend maybe won't be
another little gimme-fill-my-belly
next year while you out in the fields.
Hear me. You imagine real good
because your daddy a hammer.
Hard-time nail in his pants.
He feel wood beneath him,
he got to drive it home.

JERICHO

The question mark in my belly kicks me
as I push back the sheet, watching you undress.
You put on the black mask and lie on your side.
I open the small sack of peppermint sticks
you always bring and take one out.
I suck it as you rub my shoulders, breasts,
then with one hand, round the hollow beneath,
carved by seven months of pregnancy,
stopping when your palm covers my navel.
You groan as I slide the peppermint across my lips.

So I'm just fifteen, but I've seen others like you:
afraid, apologizing because they need something
maybe nobody else does.
You candy man, handing out the money, the sweets,
ashamed to climb your ladder of trouble.
Don't be. Make it to the top.
You'll find a ram's horn there.
Blow it seven times, yell goddamn
and watch the miniature hells below you
all fall down.

THE MORTICIAN'S TWELVE-YEAR-OLD SON

Lady, when you were alive
I'd see you on the streets,
the long green dress with the velvet flower
sewn dead center between your breasts
so tightly I could never get a look inside.

Now the gas lamps half-light the table,
washing the sheet that covers you with shadows.
A few strands of your dyed red hair
hang nearly to the floor,
as if all your blood had run there to hide.

I lift the sheet, rub the mole on your cheek
and it comes off black and oily on my hand.
I bend over your breasts and sing,
love, sister, is just a kiss away.
I cover each nipple with my mouth.
Tonight, just a kiss away.

THE GERMAN ARMY, RUSSIA, 1943

For twelve days,
I drilled through Moscow ice
to reach paradise,
that white tablecloth, set with a plate
that's cracking bit by bit
like the glassy air, like me.
I know I'll fly apart soon,
the pieces of me so light they float.
The Russians burned their crops,
rather than feed our army.
Now they strike us against each other like dry rocks
and set us on fire with a hunger
nothing can feed.
Someone calls me and I look up.
It's Hitler.
I imagine eating his terrible, luminous eyes.
Brother, he says.
I stand up, tie the rags tighter around my feet.
I hear my footsteps running after me,
but I am already gone.

TALKING TO HIS REFLECTION IN A SHALLOW POND

For Yasunari Kawabata

Chrysanthemum and nightshade:
I live on them,
though air is what I need.
I wish I could breath like you,
asleep, or even awake,
just resting your head
on the pillow wrapped in black crepe
that I brought you from Sweden.
I hoped you'd die,
your mouth open, lips dry and split,
and red like pomegranate seeds.
But now, I only want you to suffer.
I drop a stone in the pond
and it sinks through you.
Japan isn't sliding into the Pacific
this cool April morning, you are.
Yasunari Kawabata, I'm talking to you;
just drop like that stone
through your own reflection.
You stretch your lean hands toward me
and I take them.
Water covers my face, my whole head,
as I inhale myself:
cold, very cold.

Suddenly, I pull back.
For a while, I watch you struggle,
then I start walking back to my studio.
But something is wrong.
There's water everywhere
and you're standing above me.
I stare up at you from the still, clear water.
You open your mouth and I open mine.
We both speak slowly.
Brother, you deserve to suffer,
You deserve the best:
this moment, death without end.

29 (A DREAM IN TWO PARTS)

1.

Night, that old woman, jabs the sun
with a pitchfork,
and dyes the cheesecloth sky blue–violet,
as I sit at the kitchen table,
bending small pieces of wire in hoops.
You come in naked.
No. Do it yourself.

2.

I'm a nine-year-old girl,
skipping beside a single hoop of daylight.
I hear your voice.
I start running. You lift me in your arms.
I holler. The little girl turns.
Her hoop rolls out of sight.
Something warm seeps through my gown onto my belly.
She never looks back.

SHE DIDN'T EVEN WAVE

For Marilyn Monroe

I buried Mama in her wedding dress
and put gloves on her hands,
but I couldn't do much about her face,
blue-black and swollen,
so I covered it with a silk scarf.
I hike my dress up to my thighs
and rub them,
watching you tip the mortuary fan back and forth.
Hey. Come on over. Cover me all up
like I was never here. Just never.
Come on. I don't know why I talk like that.
It was a real nice funeral. Mama's.
I touch the rhinestone heart pinned to my blouse.
Honey, let's look at it again.
See. It's bright like the lightning that struck her.

I walk outside
and face the empty house.
You put your arms around me. Don't.
Let me wave goodbye.
Mama never got a chance to do it.
She was walking toward the barn
when it struck her. I didn't move;
I just stood at the screen door.
Her whole body was light.
I'd never seen anything so beautiful.

I remember how she cried in the kitchen
a few minutes before.
She said, *God. Married.*
I don't believe it, Jean, I won't.
He takes and takes and you just give.
At the door, she held out her arms
and I ran to her.
She squeezed me so tight:
I was all short of breath.
And she said, *don't do it.*
In ten years, your heart will be eaten out
and you'll forgive him, or some other man, even that
and it will kill you.
Then she walked outside.
And I kept saying, I've got to, Mama,
hug me again. Please don't go.

I C E

breaks up in obelisks on the river,
as I stand beside your grave.
I tip my head back.
Above me, the same sky you loved,
that shawl of cotton wool,
frozen around the shoulders of Minnesota.
I'm cold and so far from Texas
and my father, who gave me to you.
I was twelve, a Choctaw, a burden.
A woman, my father said, raising my skirt.
Then he showed you the roll of green gingham,
stained red, that I'd tried to crush to powder
with my small hands. I close my eyes,

and it is March 1866 again.
I'm fourteen, wearing a white smock.
I straddle the rocking horse you made for me
and stroke the black mane cut from my own hair.
Sunrise hugs you from behind,
as you walk through the open door
and lay the velvet beside me.
I give you the ebony box
with the baby's skull inside
and you set it on your work table,
comb your pale blond hair with one hand,
then nail it shut.
When the new baby starts crying, I cover my ears,

watching as you lift him from the cradle
and lay him on the pony-skin rug.
I untie the red scarf, knotted at my throat,
climb off the horse and bend over you.
I slip the scarf around your neck,
and pull it tight, remembering:
I strangled the other baby,
laid her on your stomach while you were asleep.
You break my hold and pull me to the floor.
I scratch you, bite your lips, your face,
then you cry out,
and I open and close my hands
around a row of bear teeth.

I open my eyes.
I wanted you then and now,
and I never let you know.
I kiss the headstone.
Tonight, wake me like always.
Talk and I'll listen,
while you lie on the pallet
resting your arms behind your head,
telling me about the wild rice in the marshes
and the empty .45 you call *Grace of God* that keeps you alive,
as we slide forward, without bitterness, decade by decade,
becoming transparent. Everlasting.

THE RAVINE

I wake, sweating, reach for your rosary and drop it.
I roll over on the straw and sit up. It's light out.
I pull on my pants, slip into my rope sandals
and go outside, where you sit
against a sack of beans.
I touch the chicken feathers
stuck to the purple splotches of salve on your stomach.
Your eyes, two tiny bowls of tar
set deep in your skull, stare straight ahead
and your skin is almost the color of your eyes,
because Death pressed his black face against yours.
I put our daughter in your lap,
lift you both and walk to the ravine's edge.
I step over —

— the years fly up in my face like a fine gray dust.
I'm twenty. I buy you with matches, a mirror and a rifle.
You don't talk. While I ride the mule downhill,
you walk beside me in a blue cotton dress.
Your flat Indian face shines with boar grease.
Your wide feet sink deep in the spring mud.
You raise your hands to shade your eyes
from the sudden explosion of sunlight
through the umber clouds.
In that brightness, you separate into five stained-glass women.
Four of you are floating north, south, east and west.
I reach out, shatter you in each direction.

I start to fall, catch myself,
get off the mule and make you ride.
You cry silently, ashamed to let me walk.
At bottom, you look back.
I keep going. Up a few yards,
I strip two thin pieces of bark off a tamarisk tree,
and we chew on them, sweetening the only way home.

GUADALAJARA CEMETERY

You sort the tin paintings
and lay your favorite in my lap.
Then you stroke my bare feet
as I lean against a tombstone.
It's time to cross the border
and cut your throat with two knives:
your wife, your son.
I won't try to stop you.
A cow with a mouth at both ends
chews hell going and coming.
I never asked less.
You, me, these withered flowers,
so many hearts tied in a knot,
given and taken away.

GUADALAJARA HOSPITAL

I watch the orderly stack the day's dead:
men on one cart, women on the other.
You sit two feet away, sketching
and drinking tequila.
I raise my taffeta skirt above the red garter,
take out the pesos
and lay them beside you.
I don't hold out on you.
I shove my hand under my skirt,
find the damp ten-dollar bill.
You're on top. You call the shots.
You said we'd make it here and we have.
I make them pay for it.

Later, we walk close,
smoking from one cigarette
until it's gone. I take your arm.
Next stop *end of the line*. You pull me to you
and push your tongue deep in my mouth.
I bite it. We struggle. You slap me.
I lean over the hood of the car.
You clamp a handkerchief between your teeth,
take the pesos and ten-dollar bill from your pocket
and tear them up.
Then you get in the car
and I slide in beside you.

When we finally cross the border,
I stare out the back window.
The Virgin Mary's back there
in her husband Mendoza's workroom.
She's sitting on a tall stool,
her black lace dress rolled up above her knees,
the red pumps dangling from her feet,
while he puts the adz to a small coffin;
a psalm of hammer and emptiness
only the two of them understand.
You say, *sister, breathe with me.*
We're home, now, home.
But I reach back, back through the window.
Virgin Mary, help me. Save me.
Tear me apart with your holy, invisible hands.

THE KID

My sister rubs the doll's face in mud,
then climbs through the truck window.
She ignores me as I walk around it,
hitting the flat tires with an iron rod.
The old man yells for me to help hitch the team,
but I keep walking around the truck, hitting harder,
until my mother calls.
I pick up a rock and throw it at the kitchen window,
but it falls short.
The old man's voice bounces off the air like a ball
I can't lift my leg over.

I stand beside him, waiting, but he doesn't look up
and I squeeze the rod, raise it, his skull splits open.
Mother runs toward us. I stand still,
get her across the spine as she bends over him.
I drop the rod and take the rifle from the house.
Roses are red, violets are blue,
one bullet for the black horse, two for the brown.
They're down quick. I spit, my tongue's bloody;
I've bitten it. I laugh, remember the one out back.
I catch her climbing from the truck, shoot.
The doll lands on the ground with her.
I pick it up, rock it in my arms.
Yeah. I'm Jack, Hogarth's son.
I'm nimble, I'm quick.

In the house, I put on the old man's best suit
and his patent leather shoes.
I pack my mother's satin nightgown
and my sister's doll in the suitcase.
Then I go outside and cross the fields to the highway.
I'm fourteen. I'm a wind from nowhere.
I can break your heart.

ALMOST GROWN

I swing up on the sideboard of the old car. I'm wearing
the smell of hay better than I do these starched coveralls,
my dead father's shirt, patched under each arm, and the
underwear I bought especially for today. Mother says nothing,
just watches me and sucks on her unlit pipe. My sister,
still too young to get away, wipes away a few tears with the end
of her blue apron. The red bitch runs behind yapping, then
veers into the charred field, where she chases her tail
and, building speed, makes wider and wider circles, until
she is just a streak of fire, finally burning herself to a quick stop.

I get off at the feed store. The old men playing cards ignore me.
It's Saturday afternoon. I carry the cardboard box that holds my
things under one arm, swinging the other. I see Jake the Bootlegger's
car, parked in front of the café. When I'm close, the sun
strikes its gray steel with a hammer and I have to shade my eyes
from the glare. I grope for the door, then stagger inside. The
cooler rattles a welcome. Mae, the waitress, hollers from the
kitchen, but I can't make out what she says. I sit on a stool with
the box propped up beside me.

Suddenly, Jake comes out and Mae follows him. He winks at me.
I stare through Mae's sheer nylon blouse at her lace bra. She
takes my order and I watch her as she walks to the far end of the
counter, where Jake sits, waiting, twisting the long gold chain
of his watch. I grunt with satisfaction. Good I moved, left the
farm to finish dying without me. I take out my ten-dollar bill,

rub it, feeling all the things I can buy with it: a striped tie,
one more box of cigars, a room for a week at the hotel. Hell!
It's great. Two more days and I start work at the gas station.
I take a big bite out of the hamburger Mae has set on the counter.

Jake gets up, Mae reaches for him. He shakes his head and
walks outside. She goes into the kitchen, and soon I hear her crying.
I hesitate, then follow her. She's lying on a cot, jammed against
the wall. I bend over her and she lifts her hand and touches me
the way no one ever has. I'm clumsy, but it gets done, same as
anything, I guess. She shoves me, cursing. Money, she wants
money. I'm nervous, I clutch the ten, then throw it at her. I run,
grabbing my box. In the street again, the heat, my empty pockets
heavy, as if filled with coins. At the gas station, I slip into the
Men's room and bolt the door. I sit on the dusty toilet and lean
back against the tank. Shit! I'm not through yet. I heard this
somewhere and it's true, it's got to be: you can't tell a shotgun
or a man what to do.

THE EXPECTANT FATHER

The skin of my mouth, chewed raw, tastes good.
I get up, cursing, and find the bottle of Scotch.
My mouth burns as darkess, lifting her skirt,
reveals daylight, a sleek left ankle.
The woman calls. I don't answer.
I imagine myself coming up to my own door,
holding a small reed basket in my arms.
Inside it, there is a child,
with clay tablets instead of hands,
and my name is written on each one.
The woman calls me again and I go to her.
She reaches for me, but I move away.
I frown, pulling back the covers to look at her.
So much going on outside;
the walls could cave in on us any time, any time.
I bring my face down
where the child's head should be and press hard.
I feel pain, she's pulling my hair.
I rise up, finally, and back away from the bed,
while she turns on her side
and drags her legs up to her chest.
I wait for her to cry,
then go into the kitchen.
I fix a Scotch and sit down at the table.
In six months, it is coming, in six months,
and I have no weapon against it.

SLEEP LIKE A HAMMER

I rub the hammer I use to slaughter stock
with coconut oil,
while you sit, staring at your feet, clucking,
though you've bent your head
so I can't see your lips.
The night the barn burned down,
I was crazy for help,
but you just sat on the porch
with your shoes in your lap.
I grabbed them and ran
and when I threw them into the fire,
you went in after them.
I had to drag you out
and beat out the flames.
Now you just sit,
every so often lifting your hands
as if they were holding broken glass,
and I don't know what to do, father,
I know you're thinking about your shoes
and I go on oiling, oiling,
because it's not good to let blood
harden in the cracks,
though the cows, the hogs don't care,
even I don't. I just worry like a woman.
I need something to do.
When I was fifteen, you took the pregnant hound
hunting at flood time and she didn't come back.

You said she was no good anyway
and I kicked you hard.
You took the shovel from the barn
and smashed my leg. I still limp.
I raise the hammer.
I hear my wife yelling.
She's running toward me,
bucket in one hand, the eggs in it
sloshing over the top;
huge white drops of water.
But she's in another country.
There's only you. Me.
When I bring the hammer down,
your toes splay out, snap off like burned bacon.
Your lips pull back
and your tongue drifts over your teeth
and I'm moving up to your hands, shoulders, neck, face.
Lord, moving up.

FATHER AND SON

THE MAN:
The priest and the old women
drag themselves over the hill,
as if bearing up a tiny coffin.
I look at you and the boy,
stretched out on the ground,
then back at them.
Their feet catch fire in the sunset.
Night is coming, shouldering a sack of misdeeds
that glow in the dark. Night and the carnival.
Night and the Devil.
I wipe the sweat from my face
and put on my Devil costume:
red shirt, red pants and the cotton mask.
I get the whip I keep under the pile of rocks
and strike the air with it.
When you wake, turning over on your back,
you hiss and hit your chest three times.
Keep quiet, woman. I strike the air again;
its ten-year-old hands, genitals, feet.

THE WOMAN:
I get up, pull on my burlap dress
and lift the lid off the papier-mâché coffin
you've laid across two sawhorses.
In it lies a porcelain doll,

wearing a baptismal dress.
I was pregnant when I told you
burn a doll each year
and the tenth year the boy will catch fire,
will burn away, not even leaving smoke behind.
You believed it, the way you believe
misery's a clock nobody can't walk,
that it's half past I've got,
or a quarter to got to get a shoe, get a shoe,
before the price of leather goes up.
But I say misery's another man's child.
Like this one. Francisco's son, not yours.
Francisco I took to bed,
Francisco who left Villa in 1917
and left me, too, there in the camp
and who, when you finally caught him,
heard my name and turned his pockets inside out.
He's coming tonight, after confession,
one ride on the ferris wheel
and a few drinks. He'll come.

THE MAN:
I never believed anything you said.
You had two men who now are nothing but shadows,
and soon only black like this doll's sockets.
That's what I believe in, the black.

81

Only the black forgets, so I wait.
I tend your garden of evil and watch it ripen.
Wake the boy. Go on, call him: Baby Bones, Baby Bones.
When you shake him, his head twists,
fear's wood slides under his fingernails,
he turns his round face to me and I almost reach for him.
When he gets up, I give him his costume: red shirt,
red pants, a mask.
He puts them on and I start the fire.
I never believed anything you said.

THE WOMAN:
The boy's an ape. If you look at him all the time
like I do, you see there's nothing human about him.
Francisco knows: that's why he comes,
to see for himself how his little ape grows and grows
like an ear of rainbow-colored corn,
after twelve long months of invisible rain,
rain that burns.
Sin: eat with it, sleep with it,
dress it up like the Devil.
He's still an ape.

THE MAN:
You don't know, woman. You don't know.
Everyday he's here, another man's son,

calling me father, making mud bricks with me.
Honor thy father, they say, but I say curse him.
Son of a bitch and son of a bastard,
that's what a father is. I tell him that.
Don't call me father, I say. I'm not,
you know who is.
I used to have you beat him for it
Father, he'd cry, *help me.*
Always the same.
Francisco won't come.
I saw him yesterday, in the village,
spitting blood again. And there, at his throat
the eruption of hair you find so beautiful.
I wanted to press my face in it, to bite deep,
but I held back.
He spat one last time, right at my feet,
and he walked away with his donkey
and one chicken in a cage.
I could have killed him.
Instead, my rage stabs at his back
again and again, and misses,
because it is going into the black,
where nothing touches nothing.
It starts with a toe and crawls up,
eating the shadow,
its fragments of sentences, match-heads, hope.
Here's the coffin. Go ahead, burn it.

You throw it into the fire.
I laugh. The boy dances and I follow him,
'round and 'round, two black tops on fire,
spinning under a sky full of firecrackers and stars,
letting fall a few handkerchiefs of light.

I CAN'T GET STARTED

For Ira Hayes

1. Saturday Night

A coyote eats chunks of the moon,
the night hen's yellow egg,
while I lie drunk, in a ditch.
Suddenly, a huge combat boot
punches a hole through the sky
and falls toward me.
I wave my arms. Get back.
It keeps coming.

2. Sunday Morning

I stumble out of the ditch
and make it to the shack.
I shoot a few holes in the roof,
then stare at the paper clippings of Iwo Jima.
I remember raising that rag
of red, white and blue,
afraid that if I let go, I'd live.
The bullets never touched me.
Nothing touches me.

Around noon, I make a cup of coffee
and pour a teaspoon of pepper in it
to put the fire out.
I hum between sips

and when I finish, I hug myself.
I'm burning from the bottom up,
a bottle of flesh,
kicked across the hardwood years.
I pass gin and excuses from hand to mouth,
but it's me. It's me.
I'm the one dirty habit
I just can't break.

HE KEPT ON BURNING

1. Spain, 1929

In the café, the chandelier hangs from the ceiling
by a thick rope. I'm seventeen, still a boy.
I put my hand in my lap and twist my class
ring 'round and 'round the little finger. The Basque,
toad in torn breeches and burlap vest, plays the guitar.
I look toward the stairs. The man is there, his hand
on the wooden railing. He's naked, except for the white
kimono with black cranes painted on it, and the brown pumps
with taps on each heel. I take a slice of salami, swallow
without chewing much. He comes to me, shaking his hips
as the guitar grows louder, leans down and lets me rub
a glassful of wine across his hard, rose-colored nipples.
Then he turns, taps his feet and the others clap their hands.
I take the cheese knife, slap it down on the table. He stomps,
right foot, left, one-two, one-two-three, back toward me on the
third step. He laughs, touches my lips and I sing,
Und der haifisch der hat zahne. The others watch me.
Trembling, I move to the door. I'm not one of you.
I back into the street, cursing. I slam my fist against the wall.
It doesn't bleed. The door opens, the kimono is thrown outside.
I pick it up, smell it. On the train back to Germany, that smell
and a voice whispering, dance with me baby,
all night long.

2. Buchenwald, 1945

Joseph, you move beneath the blankets. I uncover you
and hold the glass of brandy to your mouth. Your eyes open.
Wake up, Jew, drink with me, eat some of the fine German
cake my mother sent. You take the glass and drink.
I put a small piece of cake in my mouth. I taste something:
a man, a country, Schmuel Meyer, Jenny Towler, Alphonse
Glite, seven children, metal. I squeeze my eyes shut. We
leave today. Am I shaking? I do shake, don't I. I stare
through the window at the last group of prisoners,
patchwork quilt, embroidered with the letters *SS*.
It is drizzling now four days and each man, cloth dipped
in useless dye, is running into the mud at his feet.
I turn my hands up; the palms are almost smooth.
I hear the shots. I keep looking at my hands.
When I was seventeen, Joseph, when I was seventeen,
I put out a fire, but it kept on burning.

3. Peru, 1955

Midnight bleeds through the window
as you walk to the table
and drink warm beer from a tin mug.
I sniff the sausages you've laid beside the boiled eggs
and hard bread. Are they as old as that time
I told you *come with me*? You'd love me, you said.

Yes, you and guilt, tabernacle of gold teeth
and the cantor inside singing over and over, *thou shalt not*.
I take your wrist; so thin, Joseph. Suicide? — no.
There's always the boy, always,
and a kimono that smells like orange blossoms.
And hurting; twenty-six years on a razor's edge.
And I want more. More.

You lean close, stroke my chest.
Forget; yes.

Just bite me, bite me. Don't let go.

THE WOMAN WHO KNEW TOO MUCH

I plait Carmen's hair tightly,
smelling the odor of straw
she takes with her everywhere.
Then I fasten the earrings in her ears,
the ones I made
that are orange,
like the inside of her mouth
when she's been drinking rum.

When the killer comes for her,
because she won't fight,
because she knows too much —
our guns, our weakness —
she offers him rum.
His mustache of two cigars gleams.

Later, I bury her,
then slip down into the valley
to wait for reinforcements.
I eat the yams she fried for me
and when I'm done,
I feel as if I've been sleeping.

Near sunrise, I see them:
five men and two women.
They want freedom on their own terms.
But it isn't like that.

They'll find out as Carmen did.
I go to meet them.
They think they've brought me everything I need
and now I'll tell them like all the others
that they are right.
Line up, you bastards,
so I can take a closer look.
Tonight I let my woman die.
She also had arms, legs, fingers,
all the unimportant things.
I don't want to forget. I won't let you.
Go ahead, strut around,
talk, fire your guns.
But don't tell me about freedom.
Just let me see his face.

THE SINGERS

1.

You lift a piece of meat to your mouth
with the silver fork
you took from the burning house.
It glitters in your hand,
a sliver of light on mud.
Don't leave me, woman, not now.
I smell the shit odor of fear again
like the night five years ago
when I crossed the Rio Grande into Texas.
The Carranzistas had killed Zapata
and they'd kill me too, if I stayed in Chihuahua.
But half a mile in, I saw him:
Zapata on the ground in front of me.
He bowed and danced slowly around his sombrero,
and the bullet holes in his body,
black, eight-pointed stars,
gave off a luminous darkness.

Back in Mexico, I don't remember riding,
only standing beside my horse
outside a whitewashed house.
When I looked through the window,
I saw you and your father, Indian, like me,
sitting at a table, bare, except for a silver fork.
Help me, I said. *I rode with Zapata.*

But neither of you moved.
You started singing: *Zapata, Zapata, your blood is so red.*
Zapata, Zapata, you're dead.
Who's at the window, a ghost, a ghost, only a ghost.
And when I lifted my hands,
they were transparent,
my bones, colorless light.
I struck the window,
they shattered
and I smelled fear again. I could see it:
the black outline of a horse on its hind legs,
a zero burning on its belly,
burning for me, Rosebud Morales.
I screamed, screamed my name
until I came back to myself
and could see my hands, their russet skin,
wrapping some straw in a ball.
I set it afire and threw it into the house.
When you ran out, I grabbed you.
You stabbed me with the fork, but I held on.
You kept singing while your father burned.

2.

You wrap the Spanish Bible you can't read
in your shawl,
then you start running.

But I catch you by your braids,
drag you to the cooking fire and push your head in it.
When I let go, you stagger up
wearing a halo of flames.
Come on, sing with me: *Zapata, Zapata, your blood is so red.*
Sing, goddamnit. You fall.
The shadow of a train rises from your body
and lightning zigzags from the smokestack.
The smokestack is a man. Zapata. I raise my pistol.
I'm not afraid of any sonofabitch on two feet.
I fire, then jam the barrel in my mouth.
Not even you, motherfucker, not even you.

PENTECOST

For Myself

Rosebud Morales, my friend,
before you deserted,
you'd say anyone can kill an Indian
and forget it the same instant,
that it will happen to me, Emiliano Zapata.
But my men want more corn for tortillas,
more pigs, more chickens, more chilis
and land.
If I haven't got a gun or a knife,
I'll fight with a pitchfork or a hoe,
to take them from the bosses,
those high-flying birds,
with the pomade glistening on their hair,
as they promenade into their coffins.
And if I'm killed, if we're all killed right now,
we'll go on, the true Annunciation.

Rosebud, how beautiful this day is.
I'm riding to meet Guajardo.
He'll fight with me now,
against Carranza.
When I get to the hacienda, it's quiet.
Not many soldiers,
a sorrel horse, its reins held
by a woman in a thin, white American dress
and Guajardo standing on a balcony.

I get off my horse and start up the steps.
My legs burn, my chest,
my jaw, my head.
There's a hill in front of me;
it's slippery, I have to use my hands to climb it.
At the top, it's raining fire and blood
on rows and rows of black corn.
Machetes are scattered everywhere.
I grab one and start cutting the stalks.
When they hit the ground,
they turn into men.
I yell at them.
You're damned in the cradle,
in the grave, even in Heaven.
Dying doesn't end anything.
Get up. Swing those machetes.
You can't steal a man's glory
without a goddamned fight.
Boys, take the land, take it; it's yours.
If you suffer in the grave,
you can kill from it.

THE GILDED MAN

In 1561, on an expedition down the Marañon and
Amazon to find El Dorado, Lope de Aguirre killed
Urzúa, the leader of the expedition, then scores of
others. He declared rebellion against Spain and set
out to conquer Peru, *con el alma en los dientes*, with
his soul between his teeth.

1. The Orinoco, 1561

For a while today, the rafts almost float side by side.
The river is as smooth and soft
as the strip of emerald velvet
sewn around the hem of your dress, my daughter.
I call you Vera Cruz,
because you are the true cross
from which I hang by ropes of gold.
The word *father*, a spear of dark brown hair,
enters my side and disintegrates,
leaving me whole again,
smelling of quinces and gunpowder
and your stale, innocent breath.
What is it?
you whisper. I take your hand
and we walk into the jungle.
I watch you raise your dress, bend,
then tear your petticoat with your teeth.
You fold the torn cloth
and slide it between your legs.
Then you hold out your bloody hands

and I wipe them on my shirt,
already red from fighting.
Urzúa is dead. Guzmán is dead. There is no Spain.
I'm hunting El Dorado, the Gilded Man.
When I catch him. I'll cut him up.
I'll start with his feet
and give them to you to wear as earrings.
Talk to me.
I hear nothing but the monkeys squealing above me.
I point my arquebus at a silhouette in the trees, and fire.
For a moment, I think it's you falling toward me,
your dress shredding to sepia light.
I drop the arquebus and stretch out my hands.
Fall, darling, fall into me.
Lope de Aguirre. I hear my name
as I lift you in my arms.
Daughter. Beautiful.
You weigh no more than ashes.

2. Barquisimeto, Venezuela, October 27, 1561

Today it rained vengefully and hard
and my men deserted me.
My kingdom was as close
as calling it by name. Peru.
I braid your hair, daughter,
as you kneel with your head in my lap.

I talk softly, stopping to press your face to my chest.
Vera Cruz. Listen. My heart is speaking.
I am the fishes, the five loaves.
The women, the men I killed simply ate me.
There is no dying, only living in death.
I was their salvation.
I am absolved by their hunger.
El Dorado, the kingdom of gold,
is only a tapestry I wove from their blood.
Stand up. My enemies will kill me
and they won't be merciful with you.
I unsheathe my dagger. Your mouth opens.
I can't hear you. I want to. Tell me you love me.
You cover your mouth with your hands.
I stab you, then fall beside your body.
Vera Cruz. See my skin covered with gold dust
and tongues of flame,
transfigured by the pentecost of my own despair.
I, Aguirre the wanderer, Aguirre the traitor,
the Gilded Man.
Does God think that because it rains in torrents
I am not to go to Peru and destroy the world?
God. The boot heel an inch above your head is mine.
God, say your prayers.